The Angel of the Lord

Who Is He?

By Kenneth March

Copyright © 2023 by Kenneth March

The Angel of the Lord — Who Is He?
2nd Edition
By Kenneth March

Printed in the United States of America

ISBN 978-1-7321026-3-7

Contents

Chapter 1

The Angel of the Lord — Who is He?

Millions of believers all over the world know the words of Psalm 34:7 (NIV)...

> *"The angel of the Lord encamps around those who fear him, and he delivers them."*

Hand carved wooden plaques with this verse are often offered to international tourists as souvenirs. Yet I've never heard anyone ask, "Who is this angel who protects us and whom we are to fear (stand in awe and respect of). When asked, very few know who he is.

The Old Testament portion of the Bible speaks frequently about the angel of the Lord. Not <u>an</u> angel of the Lord, but <u>the</u> angel of the Lord. Who is he? And why do most Bible believing Christians know little or nothing about him?

References to **the angel of the Lord** appear at least 70 times in the Old Testament. He is not specifically mentioned even once in the New Testament. Some ask...
- What happened to him?
- Where is he now?
- What was his role?
- How powerful is he?
- Could he be Michael the archangel?

The Angel of the Lord — Who Is He?

This is not a mystery novel. I have no desire to keep you in suspense until the final chapter. **The angel of the Lord is the second person of the Holy Trinity!** If you have doubts about this, they should be gone after reading chapter 4.

He has other names as well:
Jesus; the Messiah; the Lion of Judah; the Son of Man; the Son of God; the Savior of the World; God with Us.

I believe that after reading *The angel of the Lord — Who is he?* you will share a deeper understanding and appreciation for the role of the second person of the Trinity...the one known in the Bible as the shepherd and protector of the nation of Israel throughout the Old Testament, his mission to earth as the promised messiah (savior), and his future role as the judge of humankind when he returns to earth and the people he created… and for whom he died.

> *"Who, being in very nature God, did not consider equality with God something to be used to his own advantage; rather, he made himself nothing by taking the very nature of a servant, being made in human likeness." - Philippians 2:6-7 (NIV)*

He came to pay the penalty for our sins so that sinful human beings and the holy God could be reconciled. Or, as stated in what is perhaps the best known of all Bible verses...

> *"For God so loved the world that he gave his one and only Son, that whoever believes in him shall not perish but have eternal life." - John 3:16 (NIV)*

Interestingly, characters in the Old Testament knew that the angel of the Lord was God; however, when he appeared to them, they were often confused and frightened because they had been taught that no human being can see God and live. I presume this came from God's conversation with Moses relayed in the Old Testament book of Exodus, chapter 33. Moses asked to see God. God responded by saying he would have his glory pass before Moses...

> *"But," he said, "...you cannot see my face, for no one may see me and live." - Ex. 33:20 (NIV)*

The one speaking was God the Father. Jesus, the second person of the Trinity, confirmed this...

> *"No one has seen the Father except the one who is from God; only he has seen the Father." - John 6:46 (NIV)*

Of course, here he was speaking of himself; he is the one who came from God the Father. You may have the same question I have. Why can't anyone see the Father and live? I don't think he is shy. I can't imagine that he chooses to deprive us of knowing him better. I suspect the answer may be that our mortal bodies could not physically stand being in the presence of such power.

I'm sure you have heard of the big bang theory that says that our entire universe came about instantaneously, from nothing (or an infinitesimal speck of matter)! I understand that even many Christian scientists agree with that theory. What kind of power would be needed to instantly create the billions of galaxies that scientists say are out there?

The earth is approximately 93 million miles from the sun, a
relatively small star in the universe. If we attempted to move
closer, the energy and heat from the sun would quickly make us
crispy critters. We are told there is one star, Antares, that is 10,000
times brighter than our sun and has a radius 850 times greater. So
why would we imagine we could stand in the presence of the
power source (God) that created trillions of suns (stars) instantly,
from nothing? Just a thought; perhaps St. Paul was alluding to this
when he wrote...

> God, the blessed and only Ruler, the King of kings
> and Lord of lords, who alone is immortal and who
> lives in unapproachable light, whom no one has seen
> or can see. - 1 Timothy 6:15-16 (NIV)

Keeping an Open Mind

I am reasonably sure that every person reading this book will find
some things that call into question long-held beliefs. This book
was not intended for new Christians who know little or nothing
about theology. It is intended for more mature Christians who seek
to expand their understanding of Scripture. That is not to suggest
that each and every one of *my* theological conclusions is correct.
Spirit filled believers can differ in their interpretations. No one has
a monopoly on the exegesis of God's Word.

I urge the reader to do his or her best to keep an open mind. Many,
if not most of the beliefs most Christians hold, came to us by way
of other people, and often they are not supported by the Bible. If
you believe, as I do, that the Holy Bible is the inspired Word of
God, then we must base our beliefs and doctrines solely on the
Word and not on what other humans have told us. We must ask

ourselves, "Does what I believe in this area come solely from God's Word, or did some or all of it come from human beings?"

Those with considerable theological training may be the most challenged by some of the things presented in this book. They may have had scholarly professors, whom they greatly respected, who taught them things they accepted as truth without personally verifying that they were backed by Scripture. I have tried not to state anything in this book as a fact unless it is indisputably backed by one or more Bible scriptures. That's why about half of this book is Bible verses supporting the thoughts being advanced.

I have primarily used the New International Version (NIV) and the New Living Translation (NLT) when quoting Scriptures. I do, however occasionally also quote from the English Standard Version (ESV) for its sometimes more precise translation, even though it tends to be a little less reader friendly.

Are the Persons of the Trinity Co-equal?

A great many Christians have been told that the three persons of the Trinity, Father, Son and Holy Spirit, are co-equal in every way. Many books and articles have been written on the subject of the Trinity. You can read it confidently declared that the persons of the Trinity are co-equal, co-eternal and consubstantial. You can read that the Father *generates*, the Son is *begotten* and the Holy Spirit *proceeds*. The authors of these books and articles usually have the humility to say that no human being, not even they, can understand the concept of three persons being one God.

The Angel of the Lord — Who Is He?

My credentials may not be as impressive as some of the luminaries who have written on the subject, but I know that <u>nowhere</u> does the Bible clearly support *any* of the above assertions about the Trinity.

You may have recited the words of the Athanasian Creed in church. It was written in A.D. 325. It goes on and on about how each person of the Trinity is equal in every way. Keep in mind that these are not the words of God, they are the words of fallible men. This creed also states that the Son was begotten of the Father.

About the words 'only begotten' – It is used multiple times in the ancient King James Version (KJV) of the Bible when referring to the Son. It was derived from the Greek word *monogenes*. The word can be translated as 'only begotten,' but the meaning as used in Scripture has been vigorously debated. Perhaps that is why the translators of the New International Version (NIV) chose not to use the word 'begotten' anywhere. Instead, they use the words, 'one and only.' In John 3:16 quoted above, the King James translation calls Jesus, 'the only begotten Son of God.' 'Only begotten' and 'one and only' have entirely different meanings. The 'only begotten' Son communicates that the Son somehow came out of or was produced by God the Father, somewhat like one cell dividing into two.

Please understand, I absolutely believe that the Father is fully God, the Son is fully God and the Holy Spirit is fully God. I believe that together, the three are ONE God as the scriptures declare – which is something we mortal men and women cannot fully comprehend. However, I do not believe that, within the Godhead, they are all equal; there are too many Bible verses that have convinced me that they are not.

Does it really matter? Does it affect my salvation or yours? It doesn't! You can choose to agree or disagree. I only present the following scriptures to you so that, possibly, they may help in understanding our incomparable God:

1. (Jesus praying) *"Father, I want those you have given me to be with me where I am, and to see my glory, **the glory you have given me** because you loved me before the creation of the world." - John 17:24 (NIV).*

When someone is "given" something, it is understood that before it was given to them, they did not have it. This is basic logic that most theologians choose to ignore because it does not fit within the accepted traditions of the church. So, God the Father gave Jesus the glory he has. This can only mean that at some point in time, before the creation of the world, the Trinity did not exist because Jesus was not then a part of the Godhead.

2. *For to which of the angels did God ever say, "You are my Son; today I have become your Father"? Or again, "I will be his Father, and he will be my Son?" - Hebrew 1:5 (NIV)*

Verse 4 says, *The Son is the radiance of God's glory and the exact representation of his being, sustaining all things by his powerful word.* Verse 9 continues with, *"You* (the Son) *have loved righteousness and hated wickedness; therefore God, your God, has set you above your companions."* These verses, taken together, have brought me to conclude that God elevated the Son above his companions because he had a special love for him. His "companions" can only refer to other angels. This would explain why the Son was referred to as the Angel of the Lord throughout the Old Testament.

3. (Jesus speaking) *"But when he, the Spirit of truth, comes, he will guide you into all truth. He will not speak on his own; he will speak only what he hears, and he will tell you what is yet to come. He will glorify me because it is from me that he will receive what he will make known to you. All that belongs to the Father is mine. That is why I said the Spirit will receive from me what he will make known to you." - John 16:13 (NIV)*

This verse makes it clear that the Holy Spirit only makes known to us what God the Father and the Son have given him to speak.

It seems that, when Jesus walked the earth as a man, he was constrained by a similar limitation after he received the Holy Spirit at his baptism. He told us that he speaks only what he hears from the Father...

4. *"For I did not speak of my own accord, but the Father who sent me commanded me what to say and how to say it."*

5. (Jesus speaking) *"You heard me say, 'I am going away and I am coming back to you.' If you loved me, you would be glad that I am going to the Father, for the Father is greater than I." - John 14:28 (NIV)*

Some will say that Jesus was speaking about his human nature compared to God's nature, but it seems to me that he is saying that the Father is greater than the Son. Period.

6. (Jesus speaking) *"In that day you will ask in my name. I am not saying that I will ask the Father on your behalf. No, the Father himself loves you because you have loved me and have believed that I came from God." - John 16:26-27 (NIV)*

John 3:16 says that God sent Jesus into the world. Jesus is showing deference to the Father who sent him, and tells us it is appropriate to make our requests to the Father, not to him. Of course, he, the Father and the Holy Spirit are one, though we cannot fully comprehend that.

7. *Then the end will come, when he* (Jesus) *hands over the kingdom to God the Father after he has destroyed all dominion, authority and power. For he must reign until he has put all his enemies under his feet. The last enemy to be destroyed is death. For he "has put everything under his feet." Now when it says that "everything" has been put under him, it is clear that this does not include God himself, who put everything under Christ. When he has done this, then the Son himself will be made subject to him who put everything under him, so that God may be all in all. - 1 Corinthians 15:24-28 (NIV)*

Typically, when a verse speaks of God and does not specify Christ or the Holy Spirit, it is referring to God the Father or the full Trinity. God the Father put everything under Jesus. Jesus said so: *"All authority in heaven and earth has been given to me." - Matthew 28:18* However, at some point, Jesus will make himself subject to God the Father who gave him "all authority."

8. *But I want you to know that the head of every man is Christ, the head of woman is man, and the head of Christ is God. - 1 Corinthians 11:3*

9. *"For I have come down from heaven, not to do my own will, but the will of him who sent me." – John 6:38*

10. *Jesus said to her* (Mary Magdalene), *"Do not cling to me, for I have not yet ascended to my Father; but go to my brethren and say to them, 'I am ascending to my Father and your Father, and to my God and your God."*

Chapter 2

A Good Man, a Prophet, a Crackpot, a Con Man... or God?

Some people say that Jesus was a good man or maybe a prophet because he espoused peace and love, but they do not really accept that he was the Son of God. That conclusion is seriously and logically flawed! Jesus was either mentally unhinged and thought he was God, or a liar who conned the people into believing he was the promised Messiah, or exactly whom he claimed to be on many occasions, that is, **God**. If he was mentally disturbed or a con man, you could not call him a good man or a prophet. If he was whom he said he was, he was so much more!

I heard someone say that Jesus never claimed to be God. Not true!

Jesus claims to be God

In the first scripture that follows, Jesus makes the claim that he existed before Abraham was born hundreds of years earlier. When he was challenged on this he said, ***"...before Abraham was even born, I AM!"*** The Jews he was speaking to instantly knew he was claiming to be God because when Moses asked God whom he should say sent him to obtain the release of the Jewish people from their slavery in Egypt, God replied...

> *"I AM who I AM. Say this to the people of Israel: 'I AM has sent me to you.'" - Exodus 3:14 (NIV)*

Jesus said...

> *"And though I have no wish to glorify myself, God is going to glorify me. He is the true judge. I tell you the truth, anyone who obeys my teaching will never die!"*
>
> *The people said, "Now we know you are possessed by a demon. Even Abraham and the prophets died, but you say, 'Anyone who obeys my teaching will never die!' Are you greater than our father Abraham? He died, and so did the prophets. Who do you think you are?"*
>
> *Jesus answered, "If I want glory for myself, it doesn't count. But it is my Father who will glorify me. You say, 'He is our God,' but you don't even know him. I know him. If I said otherwise, I would be as great a liar as you! But I do know him and obey him. Your father Abraham rejoiced as he looked forward to my coming. He saw it and was glad."*
>
> *The people said, "You aren't even fifty years old. How can you say you have seen Abraham?"*
>
> *Jesus answered, "I tell you the truth, **before Abraham was even born, I AM!"** At that point they picked up stones to throw at him. But Jesus was hidden from them and left the Temple. - John 8:50-59 (NLT)*

There are many such scriptures in which Jesus said that he came from God and was God. Here are two more...

(Jesus speaking) *"My sheep listen to my voice; I know them, and they follow me. I give them eternal life, and they shall never perish; no one will snatch them out of my hand. My Father, who has given them to me, is greater than all; no one can snatch them out of my Father's hand. **I and the Father are one**." - John 10:27-30 (NIV)*

(Jesus speaking) *"Don't let your hearts be troubled. Trust in God, and trust also in me. There is more than enough room in my Father's home. If this were not so, would I have told you that I am going to prepare a place for you? When everything is ready, I will come and get you, so that you will always be with me where I am. And you know the way to where I am going."*

"No, we don't know, Lord," Thomas said. "We have no idea where you are going, so how can we know the way?"

*Jesus told him, "I am the way, the truth, and the life. No one can come to the Father except through me. **If you had really known me, you would know who my Father is. From now on, you do know him and have seen him!"***

Philip said, "Lord, show us the Father, and we will be satisfied."

*Jesus replied, "Have I been with you all this time, Philip, and yet you still don't know who I am? **Anyone who has seen me has seen the Father!** So why are you asking me to show him to you? Don't you believe that I am in the Father and the Father is in me? The words I speak are not my own, but my Father who lives in me does his work through me. Just believe that I am in the Father and the Father is in* *me. Or at least believe because of the work you have seen me do." - John 14:1-11(NLT)*

What is your verdict? Was he a crackpot, a con man, or God? There are no other choices.

Chapter 3

In the Beginning

Since this book is about the Biblical roles of the second person of the Trinity from the creation of the world to his return to earth on judgement day, it seems appropriate to start at the beginning...or at least what the Bible calls the beginning, which may simply be the beginning of the universe when God created it. We know that angels existed before the creation of the world, but beyond that what transpired before that is unknown, and apparently nothing God felt we needed to know.

> *In the beginning God created the heavens and the earth. - Genesis 1:1 (NIV)*

Chapter 1 of the Gospel of John tells us about our creator...

> *In the beginning was the Word, and the Word was with God, and the Word was God. He was with God in the beginning. Through him all things were made; without him nothing was made that has been made. - John 1:1-3*

John, the Apostle of Jesus, says that in him was life, and that life was the light of men.

> *The true light that gives light to every man was coming into the world. - John 1:9 (NIV)*

John, the Apostle, then gets more specific about who that light is...

> *The Word became flesh and lived for a while among us. We have seen his glory, the glory of the one and only Son, who came from the Father, full of grace and truth. - John 1:14 (NIV)*

> *He was in the world, and though the world was made through him, the world did not recognize him. He came to that which was his own, but his own did not receive him. - John 1:10-11 (NIV)*

Saint Paul echoes John's testimony confirming that the preincarnate Jesus is the person of the Trinity credited with the creation of the world...

> *He (Jesus) is the image of the invisible God, the firstborn over all creation. For in him all things were created: things in heaven and on earth, visible and invisible, whether thrones or powers or rulers or authorities; all things have been created through him and for him. - Colossians 1:15-16 (NIV)*

Lastly, the writer of the book of Hebrews expresses the same thoughts about the creator...

> *In the past God spoke to our ancestors through the prophets at many times and in various ways, but in these last days he has spoken to us by his Son, whom he appointed heir of all things, and through whom also he made the universe. The Son is the radiance of*

*God's glory and the exact representation of his being,
sustaining all things by his powerful word. After he
had provided purification for sins, he sat down at the
right hand of the Majesty in heaven. - Hebrews 1:1–3
(NIV)*

So, why then does the ancient Apostles Creed begin with the words, "I believe in God, the Father almighty, creator of heaven and earth?"

First, the Apostles Creed was not written by any of Jesus' twelve apostles. And second, I must presume that it was not inspired by the Holy Spirit. This creed, dating back to the fourth century A.D. was written by men who obviously did not strictly adhere to Scripture.

Certainly, the power of God the Father was at work in the creation of the world. Jesus tells us...

*"All that belongs to the Father is mine." - John 16:15
(NIV)*

However, if we are going to single out one person of the Trinity to give credit for creation, let's go with what the Bible says, and it says that all things were made through, for and by the Son, who is the second person of the Trinity.

Chapter 4

Biblical Accounts of The Angel of the Lord

I would not attempt to convince anyone that the angel of the Lord is in fact God himself, the second person of the Trinity, without the full support of scriptures. Therefore, this chapter consists, exclusively, of Bible stories that should convince even the biggest skeptic. And if the scriptures in this chapter are not enough, please see chapter 5 where you will find more scriptures supporting the fact that the angel of the Lord is God.

Moses and the Burning Bush

Now Moses was tending the flock of Jethro his father-in-law, the priest of Midian, and he led the flock to the far side of the wilderness and came to Horeb, the mountain of God. ***There the angel of the Lord appeared to him in flames of fire from within a bush.*** *Moses saw that though the bush was on fire it did not burn up. So Moses thought, "I will go over and see this strange sight—why the bush does not burn up."*

When the LORD *saw that he had gone over to look,* ***God called to him from within the bush****, "Moses! Moses!"*

And Moses said, "Here I am."

"Do not come any closer," God said. "Take off your sandals, for the place where you are standing is holy ground." Then he said, **"I am the God of your father, the God of Abraham, the God of Isaac and the God of Jacob."** *At this, Moses hid his face, because he was afraid to look at God. - Exodus 3:1-6 (NIV)*

Abraham's Faith Is Tested

Sometime later **God** *tested Abraham. He said to him... "Abraham!" "Here I am," he replied.*

Then God said, "Take your son, your only son Isaac, whom you love, and go to the region of Moriah. Sacrifice him there as a burnt offering on a mountain I will show you."

Early the next morning Abraham got up and loaded his donkey. He took with him two of his servants and his son Isaac. When he had cut enough wood for the burnt offering, he set out for the place God had told him about. On the third day Abraham looked up and saw the place in the distance. He said to his servants, "Stay here with the donkey while I and the boy go over there. We will worship and then we will come back to you."

Abraham took the wood for the burnt offering and placed it on his son Isaac, and he himself carried the fire and the knife. As the two of them went on together, Isaac spoke up and said to his father Abraham, "Father?"

"Yes, my son?" Abraham replied.

"The fire and wood are here," Isaac said, "but where is the lamb for the burnt offering?"

Abraham answered, "God himself will provide the lamb for the burnt offering, my son." And the two of them went on together.

*When they reached the place God had told him about, Abraham built an altar there and arranged the wood on it. He bound his son Isaac and laid him on the altar, on top of the wood. Then he reached out his hand and took the knife to slay his son. But **the angel of the Lord called out to him from heaven**, "Abraham! Abraham!"*

"Here I am," he replied.

*"Do not lay a hand on the boy," he said. "Do not do anything to him. Now I know that you fear God, because you have not withheld **from me** your son, your only son."*

Abraham looked up and there in a thicket he saw a ram caught by its horns. He went over and took the ram and sacrificed it as a burnt offering instead of his son. So Abraham called that place The LORD Will Provide. And to this day it is said, "On the mountain of the LORD it will be provided."

***The angel of the Lord called to Abraham from heaven** a second time and said, **"I swear by myself, declares the LORD**, that because you have done this and have not withheld your son, your only son, **I will surely bless you** and make your descendants as numerous as the stars in the sky and as the sand on*

the seashore. Your descendants will take possession
of the cities of their enemies, and through your
offspring all nations on earth will be blessed, because
*you have obeyed **me**." - Genesis 22:1-18 (NIV)*

Sarai's Runaway Servant Girl

Now Sarai, Abram's wife, had borne him no children.
She had a female Egyptian servant whose name was
Hagar. And Sarai said to Abram, "Behold now, the
LORD has prevented me from bearing children. Go in
to my servant; it may be that I shall obtain children
by her." And Abram listened to the voice of Sarai. So,
after Abram had lived ten years in the land of
Canaan, Sarai, Abram's wife, took Hagar the
Egyptian, her servant, and gave her to Abram her
husband as a wife. And he went in to Hagar, and she
conceived. And when she saw that she had conceived,
she looked with contempt on her mistress. And Sarai
said to Abram, "May the wrong done to me be on
you! I gave my servant to your embrace, and when
she saw that she had conceived, she looked on me
with contempt. May the LORD judge between you and
me!" But Abram said to Sarai, "Behold, your servant
is in your power; do to her as you please." Then
Sarai dealt harshly with her, and she fled from her.

***The angel of the LORD** found her by a spring of water*
in the wilderness, the spring on the way to Shur. And

*he said, "Hagar, servant of Sarai, where have you come from and where are you going?" She said, "I am fleeing from my mistress Sarai." The angel of the LORD said to her, "Return to your mistress and submit to her." The angel of the LORD also said to her, "**I will surely multiply your offspring** so that they cannot be numbered for multitude." And the angel of the LORD said to her, "Behold, you are pregnant and shall bear a son. You shall call his name Ishmael, because the LORD has listened to your affliction. He shall be a wild donkey of a man, his hand will be against everyone and everyone's hand against him, and he will live in hostility toward all his brothers." **So she called the name of the LORD who spoke to her, "You are a God of seeing," for she said, "Truly here I have seen him who looks after me."** - Genesis 16:1-13 (ESV)*

Gideon is Chosen to Deliver God's People

The angel of the Lord *came and sat down under the oak in Ophrah that belonged to Joash the Abiezrite, where his son Gideon was threshing wheat in a winepress to keep it from the Midianites. When the angel of the Lord appeared to Gideon, he said, "The LORD is with you, mighty warrior."*

"Pardon me, my lord," Gideon replied, "but if the LORD is with us, why has all this happened to us? Where are all his wonders that our ancestors told us

25

about when they said, 'Did not the LORD bring us up out of Egypt?' But now the LORD has abandoned us and given us into the hand of Midian."

*The LORD turned to him and said, "Go in the strength you have and save Israel out of Midian's hand. **Am I not sending you?**"*

"Pardon me, my lord," Gideon replied, "but how can I save Israel? My clan is the weakest in Manasseh, and I am the least in my family."

*The LORD answered, "**I will be with you**, and you will strike down all the Midianites, leaving none alive."*

Gideon replied, "If now I have found favor in your eyes, <u>give me a sign that it is really you talking to me</u>. Please do not go away until I come back and bring my offering and set it before you."

And the LORD said, "I will wait until you return."

Gideon went inside, prepared a young goat, and from an ephah of flour he made bread without yeast. Putting the meat in a basket and its broth in a pot, he brought them out and offered them to him under the oak.

The angel of God said to him, "Take the meat and the unleavened bread, place them on this rock, and pour out the broth." And Gideon did so. Then the angel of the Lord touched the meat and the unleavened bread with the tip of the staff that was in his hand. Fire flared from the rock, consuming the meat and the bread. And the angel of the Lord disappeared.

When Gideon realized that it was the angel of the Lord, he exclaimed, "Alas, Sovereign LORD! I have seen the angel of the Lord face to face!"

But the LORD said to him, "Peace! Do not be afraid. You are not going to die."

So Gideon built an altar to the LORD there and called it The LORD Is Peace. To this day it stands in Ophrah of the Abiezrites. - Judges 6:11-24 - (NIV)

The Birth of Samson

*A certain man of Zorah, named Manoah, from the clan of the Danites, had a wife who was childless, unable to give birth. **The angel of the Lord appeared to her** and said, "You are barren and childless, but you are going to become pregnant and give birth to a son. Now see to it that you drink no wine or other fermented drink and that you do not eat anything unclean. You will become pregnant and have a son whose head is never to be touched by a razor because the boy is to be a Nazirite, dedicated to God from the womb. He will take the lead in delivering Israel from the hands of the Philistines."*

*Then the woman went to her husband and told him, "A man of God came to me. **He looked like an angel of God, very awesome.** I didn't ask him where he came from, and he didn't tell me his name. But he said to me, 'You will become pregnant and have a son. Now then, drink no wine or other fermented drink and do not eat anything unclean, because the*

27

boy will be a Nazirite of God from the womb until the day of his death.'"

Then Manoah prayed to the LORD: "Pardon your servant, Lord. I beg you to let the man of God you sent to us come again to teach us how to bring up the boy who is to be born."

*God heard Manoah, and **the angel of God came again** to the woman while she was out in the field; but her husband Manoah was not with her. The woman hurried to tell her husband, "He's here! The man who appeared to me the other day!"*

Manoah got up and followed his wife. When he came to the man, he said, "Are you the man who talked to my wife?"

"I am," he said.

So Manoah asked him, "When your words are fulfilled, what is to be the rule that governs the boy's life and work?"

The angel of the Lord answered, "Your wife must do all that I have told her. ¹⁴ She must not eat anything that comes from the grapevine, nor drink any wine or other fermented drink nor eat anything unclean. She must do everything I have commanded her."

Manoah said to the angel of the Lord, "We would like you to stay until we prepare a young goat for you."

The angel of the Lord replied, "Even though you detain me, I will not eat any of your food. But if you prepare a burnt offering, offer it to the LORD."

(Manoah did not realize that it was the angel of the Lord.)

Then Manoah inquired of the angel of the Lord, "What is your name, so that we may honor you when your word comes true?"

He replied, "Why do you ask my name? It is beyond understanding." Then Manoah took a young goat, together with the grain offering, and sacrificed it on a rock to the LORD. And the LORD did an amazing thing while Manoah and his wife watched: As the flame blazed up from the altar toward heaven, the angel of the Lord ascended in the flame. Seeing this, Manoah and his wife fell with their faces to the ground. When the angel of the Lord did not show himself again to Manoah and his wife, **Manoah realized that it was the angel of the Lord.**

"We are doomed to die!" he said to his wife. "We have seen God!"

But his wife answered, "If the LORD had meant to kill us, he would not have accepted a burnt offering and grain offering from our hands, nor shown us all these things or now told us this." - Judges 13:2-23 (NIV)

Balaam and His Talking Donkey

Balaam got up in the morning, saddled his donkey and went with the princes of Moab. But **God was very angry when he went, and the angel of the Lord stood in the road to oppose him**. Balaam was riding on his donkey, and his two servants were with him. When the donkey *saw the angel of the Lord standing in the road with a drawn sword in his hand, she turned off the road into a field. Balaam beat it to get it back on the road. – Numbers 22:21-23 NIV*

The angel of the Lord *asked him, "Why have you beaten your donkey these three times? I have come here to oppose you because your path is a reckless one* ***before me****. The donkey saw me and turned away from me these three times. If it had not turned away, I would certainly have killed you by now, but I would have spared her." – Numbers 22:32-33 NIV*

The Lord's Judgement on Ahaziah

But ***the angel of the Lord*** *said to Elijah the Tishbite, "Go up and meet the messengers of the king of Samaria and ask them, 'Is it because there is no God in Israel that you are going off to consult Baal-Zebub, the god of Ekron?' Therefore this is what* ***the LORD*** *says: 'You will not leave the bed you are lying on. You will certainly die!'" So Elijah went. - 2 kings 1:3-4*

An Appearance at Bokim

The angel of the Lord *went up from Gilgal to Bokim and said,* ***"I brought you up out of Egypt*** *and led you into the land I swore to give to your ancestors.* ***I said, 'I will never break my covenant with you****, and you shall not make a covenant with the people of this land, but you shall break down their altars.' Yet* ***you have disobeyed me****. Why have you done this?" – Judges 2:1-2 NIV*

Jacob Wrestles with God

> *That night Jacob got up and took his two wives, his two female servants and his eleven sons and crossed the ford of the Jabbok. After he had sent them across the stream, he sent over all his possessions. So Jacob was left alone, and a man wrestled with him till daybreak. When the man saw that he could not overpower him, he touched the socket of Jacob's hip so that his hip was wrenched as he wrestled with the man. Then the man said, "Let me go, for it is daybreak."*
>
> *But Jacob replied, "I will not let you go unless you bless me."*
>
> *The man asked him, "What is your name?"*
>
> *"Jacob," he answered.*
>
> *Then the man said, "Your name will no longer be Jacob, but Israel, because **you have struggled with God** and with humans and have overcome."*
>
> *Jacob said, "Please tell me your name." But he replied, "Why do you ask my name?" Then he blessed him there.*
>
> *So Jacob called the place Peniel, saying, "**It is because I saw God face to face**, and yet my life was spared." - Genesis 32:22-30*

This is a fascinating and unusual encounter. The prophet Hosea speaks of this event and tells us that Jacob wrestled with the Angel who is the Lord of Heaven's Armies...

*Even in the womb, Jacob struggled with his brother; when he became a man, **he even fought with God**. Yes, **he wrestled with the angel** and won. He wept and pleaded for a blessing from him. There at Bethel he met God face to face, and God spoke to him— **the LORD God of Heaven's Armies, the LORD is his name!** - Hosea 12:3-5 (NLT)*

Chapter 5

Other Appearances of the Angel of the Lord

Before the Fall of Jericho's Walls

When Joshua was by Jericho, he lifted up his eyes and looked, and behold, a man was standing before him with his drawn sword in his hand. And Joshua went to him and said to him, "Are you for us, or for our adversaries?" And he said, "No; but I am the commander of the army of the LORD. Now I have come." And Joshua fell on his face to the earth and worshiped and said to him, "What does my lord say to his servant?" [15] *And the commander of the LORD's army said to Joshua, "Take off your sandals from your feet, for the place where you are standing is holy." And Joshua did so. - Joshua 5:13-15 (ESV)*

As will be discussed in chapter 6, the Angel of the Lord is also known as the commander of the army of the Lord. Joshua was told he was standing on holy ground. He prostrated himself in worship. Angels who are not God do not accept human worship, so this was the angel of the Lord!

The Tent of Meeting

Now Moses used to take a tent and pitch it outside the camp some distance away, calling it the "tent of meeting." Anyone inquiring of the LORD would go to the tent of meeting outside the camp. And whenever Moses went out to the tent, all the people rose and

33

stood at the entrances to their tents, watching Moses until he entered the tent. As Moses went into the tent, the pillar of cloud would come down and stay at the entrance, while the LORD spoke with Moses. Whenever the people saw the pillar of cloud standing at the entrance to the tent, they all stood and worshiped, each at the entrance to their tent. ***The LORD would speak to Moses face to face, as one speaks to a friend.*** *- Exodus 33:7-11 (NIV)*

In John 6:46 Jesus tells us: *"No one has seen the Father except the one who is from God; only he has seen the Father."* Therefore, Moses was not meeting face to face with God the Father. It had to be the Son or the Holy Spirit, and the Bible never suggests that anyone has ever seen the Holy Spirit in bodily form.

God's Angel Precedes the Israelites

God the Father speaking of the angel of the Lord...

"See, ***I am sending an angel ahead of you*** *to guard you along the way and to bring you to the place I have prepared.* ***Pay attention to him and listen to what he says. Do not rebel against him; he will not forgive your rebellion,*** <u>***since my Name is in him.***</u> *If you listen carefully to what he says and do all that I say, I will be an enemy to your enemies and will oppose those who oppose you. My angel will go ahead of you and bring you into the land of the Amorites, Hittites, Perizzites, Canaanites, Hivites and Jebusites, and I will wipe them out. - Exodus 23:20-23 (NIV)*

> *By day **the LORD went ahead of them** in a pillar of cloud to guide them on their way and by night in a pillar of fire to give them light, so that they could travel by day or night. Neither the pillar of cloud by day nor the pillar of fire by night left its place in front of the people. - Exodus 13:21-22 (NIV)*

> *And they will tell the inhabitants of this land about it. They have already heard that you, LORD, are with these people and that **you, LORD, have been seen face to face,** that your cloud stays over them, and that you go before them in a pillar of cloud by day and a pillar of fire by night. - Numbers 14:14 (NIV)*

This is an excellent example of the angel of the Lord watching over the people of Israel, leading and protecting them.

King Hezekiah's Prayer

King Hezekiah ruled over the kingdom of Judah from 726-697 BC. During his reign, King Sennacherib, the ruler of the powerful Assyrian Empire sent a large army to conquer the City of Jerusalem. King Sennacherib sent a message to King Hezekiah seeking his surrender. He boasted arrogantly about his numerous conquests and said that Hezekiah would be foolish to think that the Lord could deliver Jerusalem from his hand.

> *Hezekiah received the letter from the messengers and read it. Then he went up to the temple of the LORD and spread it out before the LORD. And Hezekiah prayed to the LORD: "O LORD, God of Israel, enthroned between the cherubim, you alone are God*

over all the kingdoms of the earth. You have made heaven and earth. Give ear, O LORD, and hear; open your eyes, O LORD, and see; listen to the words Sennacherib has sent to insult the living God." - 2 Kings 19:14-16

*That night **the angel of the Lord** went out and put to death a hundred and eighty-five thousand in the Assyrian camp. When the people got up the next morning—there were all the dead bodies! So Sennacherib king of Assyria broke camp and withdrew. He returned to Nineveh and stayed there. - 2 Kings 19:35-36 (NIV)*

This is a side of the Son of God that we do not think of when we think of Jesus. Though we know Jesus as a man, he is also the all-powerful God who was not about to tolerate the blasphemies of King Sennacherib. For a perspective on the magnitude of the Assyrian army's devastation...the number of U.S. troops in Iraq following "the Surge" initiated by President George W. Bush, peaked at 157,800. Can you imagine the Assyrian General's shock the morning he rose and discovered that 185,000 of his troops were dead?

Punishment for King David's Sin

Satan rose up against Israel and incited David to take a census of Israel. So David said to Joab and the commanders of the troops, "Go and count the Israelites from Beersheba to Dan. Then report back to me so that I may know how many there are."

But Joab replied, "May the LORD multiply his troops a hundred times over. My lord the king, are they not all my lord's subjects? Why does my lord want to do this? Why should he bring guilt on Israel?"

The king's word, however, overruled Joab; so Joab left and went throughout Israel and then came back to Jerusalem. Joab reported the number of the fighting men to David: In all Israel there were one million one hundred thousand men who could handle a sword, including four hundred and seventy thousand in Judah.

But Joab did not include Levi and Benjamin in the numbering, because the king's command was repulsive to him. This command was also evil in the sight of God; so he punished Israel. - 1 Chronicles 21:1-7 (NIV)

By calling for a census to determine how many fighting men were in Israel, King David was putting his faith in the size of his fighting forces, instead of in God who had always given David and Israel victories over their enemies. This provoked the Lord to anger. Leaders who claim to know God are his representatives to the people and are held to a higher standard.

Then David said to God, "I have sinned greatly by doing this. Now, I beg you, take away the guilt of your servant. I have done a very foolish thing."

The LORD said to Gad, David's seer, "Go and tell David, 'This is what the LORD says: I am giving you three options. Choose one of them for me to carry out against you.'"

So Gad went to David and said to him, "This is what the LORD says: 'Take your choice: three years of famine, three months of being swept away before your enemies, with their swords overtaking you, or three days of the sword of the LORD - days of plague in the *land, with **the angel of the Lord** ravaging every part of Israel.' Now then, decide how I should answer the one who sent me."*

David said to Gad, "I am in deep distress. Let me fall into the hands of the LORD, for his mercy is very great; but do not let me fall into the hands of men."

So the LORD sent a plague on Israel, and seventy thousand men of Israel fell dead. And God sent an angel to destroy Jerusalem. But as the angel was doing so, the LORD saw it and relented concerning the disaster and said to the angel who was destroying the people, "Enough! Withdraw your hand." The angel of the Lord was then standing at the threshing floor of Araunah⁽ᵘ⁾ *the Jebusite.*

*David looked up and saw **the angel of the Lord standing between heaven and earth**, with a drawn sword in his hand extended over Jerusalem. Then David and the elders, clothed in sackcloth, fell facedown.*

David said to God, "Was it not I who ordered the fighting men to be counted? I, the shepherd, have sinned and done wrong. These are but sheep. What have they done? LORD my God, let your hand fall on me and my family, but do not let this plague remain on your people."

*Then **the angel of the Lord** ordered Gad to tell David to go up and build an altar to the LORD on the threshing floor of Araunah the Jebusite. So David went up in obedience to the word that Gad had spoken in the name of the LORD. - 1 Chronicles 21:8-19 (NIV)*

Chapter 6

The Commander of Heaven's Armies

Throughout the Old Testament there are numerous references to one of the persons of the Godhead who is variously called "the Lord of Hosts," "the Lord of Heaven's Armies," "the Lord of Armies," "the Lord of Heavenly forces," "the commander of all of heaven's armies," and "the Lord who commands armies," depending on the translation being read. The title is derived from the Hebrew name Jehovah Sabaoth. Sabaoth is military term meaning *hosts* or *army*.

The New International Version is the only version I know that translates the words Jehovah Sabaoth simply as "the Lord Almighty." Nevertheless, we can easily conclude that this person of the Trinity is the commander of the armies of heaven. The holder of these titles is mentioned over 260 times in the Old Testament.

> *Even in the womb, Jacob struggled with his brother; when he became a man, he even fought with God. Yes,* **he wrestled with the angel** *and won. He wept and pleaded for a blessing from him. There at Bethel he met God face to face, and God spoke to him—* **the LORD God of Heaven's Armies,** *the LORD is his name! - Hosea 12:3-5 (NLT)*

So, the angel of the Lord is the commander of Heaven's armies who identified himself that way to Joshua (see "Before the Fall of Jericho's Walls" in the previous chapter).

> *If they really are prophets and speak the Lord's messages, let them pray to **the Lord of Heaven's Armies**. Let them pray that the articles remaining in the Lord's Temple and in the king's palace and in the palaces of Jerusalem will not be carried away to Babylon! - Jeremiah 27:18 (NLT)*

> *...then hear the Lord's message to the remnant of Judah. This is what **the Lord of Heaven's Armies**, the God of Israel, says: 'If you are determined to go to Egypt and live there... - Jeremiah 42:15 (NLT)*

Is the Angel of the Lord Michael the Archangel?

Another way of phrasing that question is, is Michael, the archangel, the second person of the Trinity? Some people think so. Probably more do not, or have never even considered the question. There are a number of reasons to believe that they are same person.

First, the word archangel appears only twice in the Bible, in Jude vs. 9 and 1 Thessalonians 4:16. In the Jude reference we are told that this is Michael the archangel. While some think that 'archangel' is a category of powerful angels, we have no reason to believe, from the Bible, that there is more than one archangel.

May the Lord rebuke you

In the Jude reference (above) we are told that Michael the archangel did not presume to pronounce a blasphemous judgment against the devil, but said, "May the Lord rebuke you."

In Zechariah 3:1-2 we read that **the angel of the Lord** said the same thing to Satan, "The Lord rebuke you, Satan!"

I don't know what is to be made of this, but it is interesting that neither Michael nor the angel of the Lord felt it was their place to rebuke Satan. As you probably remember from Scriptures, Satan was known as Lucifer. He was an extremely powerful and majestic angel who became prideful and corrupt. (Ezekial 28 and Isaiah 14)

The Great Dragon, Lucifer, defeated

The first part of this chapter clarifies that the angel of the Lord is the commander of the Lord's armies. Revelation 12:7-9 tells us that Michael and his angels fought against and defeated the great dragon (also known as Satan or Lucifer) and the angels who rebelled with him. Therefore, some conclude that Michael and the angel of the Lord must be the same.

The Voice of the Archangel

In the gospel of John we read this about Jesus' end-time return to earth...

> *"I tell you the truth, a time is coming and has now come when the dead will hear **the voice of the Son of God** and those who hear will live. For as the Father has life in himself, so he has granted the Son also to*

*have life in himself. And he has given him authority to judge because he is the Son of Man. Do not be amazed at this, for a time is coming when **all who are in their graves will hear his voice and come out—** those who have done what is good will rise to live, and those who have done what is evil will rise to be condemned." – John 5:25-29*

Some translations say the Lord will come with the voice of <u>the</u> archangel, and others say with the voice of <u>an</u> archangel…

"For the Lord himself will come down from heaven, with a loud command, with the voice of <u>the archangel</u> and with the trumpet call of God, and the dead in Christ will rise first." – 1 Thessalonians 4:6 (NIV)

"For the Lord himself will descend from heaven with a cry of command, with the voice of <u>an archangel</u>, and with the sound of the trumpet of God. And the dead in Christ will rise first." – 1 Thessalonians 4:6 (ESV)

"For the Lord himself will come down from heaven with a commanding shout, with the voice of <u>the archangel</u>, and with the trumpet call of God. First, the believers who have died will rise from their graves." – 1 Thessalonians 4:6 (NLT)

Whether it is the voice of <u>the</u> archangel or <u>an</u> archangel, it appears it comes out of the mouth of the Lord, who is Jesus, who was previously known as the angel of the Lord. Since the only archangel the bible speaks of is Michael, it is not hard to understand why some use this verse to support that the angel of the Lord and Michael are the same person.

From the book of Daniel

In Daniel chapter 10, an angel comes to Daniel in response to his prayers. This angel is described by Daniel this way...

> *I looked up and there before me was a man dressed in linen, with a belt of the finest gold around his waist. His body was like chrysolite, his face like lightning, his eyes like flaming torches, his arms and legs like the gleam of burnished bronze, and his voice like the sound of a multitude. - Daniel 10:5-6 (NIV)*

This impressive angel was <u>not</u> Michael. In the verses that follow we learn that this powerful angel was somehow prevented from coming to Daniel by "the prince of Persia," probably a powerful demon, or possibly Satan himself.

This angel goes on to say, in Daniel 10:13, that Michael, **"one of the chief princes,"** came to help him so he could continue his mission to Daniel. Let's stop there for a moment. **Calling the archangel Michael *"one of the chief princes"* <u>does NOT</u> seem like it could be referring to the second person of the Trinity who is himself God and the creator of all things.**

In verse 21 this angel refers to Michael as "your prince."

Finally, in Daniel 12:1 Michael is called *"the great prince who protects your people" (NIV)* or *"who has charge of your people."*

(ESV). This **does** sound like the angel of the Lord. Bible verses I've shared with you earlier make it clear that the angel of the Lord shepherded and protected the Israelites throughout the Old Testament. He went before them in the pillar of cloud by day and in the pillar of fire at night. He is the one who met with Moses in the Tent of Meeting.

> (End-Time Prophecy) *"At that time Michael, the great prince who protects your people, will arise. There will be a time of distress such as has not happened from the beginning of nations until then. But at that time your people – everyone whose name is found written in the book – will be delivered. - Daniel 12:1 (NIV)*

So, people can speculate about whether or not Michael is the angel of the Lord (Jesus), but, in my opinion, because of the Daniel 10:13 verse above, I must conclude that Michael is **not** the angel of the Lord (Jesus).

Chapter 7

Was Jesus a Carpenter or a Stonemason?

The Greek word translated "carpenter" in the Bible is "tekton." Tekton essentially means builder, i.e. men who were masters of their craft. It would have included carpenters, stonemasons and some other trades. Current day Bible translators continue to translate tekton as "carpenter;" however, I have found that translators are wont to change a translation that has been passed down for centuries unless they have absolute proof that the original rendering was incorrect.

In the country of Haiti, which I have been to many times, nearly all buildings are constructed of concrete blocks because there are few trees that have not been harvested for making charcoal for cooking or for other purposes.

Israel has about as many trees as Haiti. It seems to make sense that they would have built with stone, not wood. I was on a tour of Israel, on a bus, and overheard the driver ask one of my fellow tourists if Israel looked like he had expected. If you had seen the terrain, you would have thought the man's answer was as funny as I did. He said, "I thought there would be more rocks." This cracked me up because as far as the eye could see there was nothing but rocks.

For this reason many believe that Joseph was more likely a stonemason, and Jesus, being trained by his father in the family business, was also a stonemason.

One might speculate that Peter was thinking of Jesus' occupation as a stone mason when he wrote...

> *As you come to him, the living Stone—rejected by humans but chosen by God and precious to him— you also, like living stones, are being built into a spiritual house to be a holy priesthood, offering spiritual sacrifices acceptable to God through Jesus Christ. - 1 Peter 2:4-5 (NIV)*

Or maybe because of Jesus' occupation, the disciples pointed out to him the huge stones of the Temple building...

> *Jesus left the temple and was walking away when his disciples came up to him to call his attention to its buildings. "Do you see all these things?" he asked. "Truly I tell you, not one stone here will be left on another; every one will be thrown down." - Matthew 24:1-2 (NIV)*

Primarily because of the scarcity of trees, it seems logical to me that Jesus was a stonemason rather than a carpenter. If you go to the internet and look at pictures of buildings in Israel, you will see my point.

Chapter 8

Jesus Was NOT Poor and Homeless

Too often I hear people say that Jesus was poor and homeless. They say he had no money and no place to sleep. As a result, some people think that being poor is a virtue. I hope to show you, from the Bible, that that is not true. God wants to bless us, and he provided for all of his Son's needs.

Let me ask you, if you were God, and you were sending your own son on a mission to earth to tell people what you are like and to die for their sins, would you provide everything that your son needs? Or would you let him sleep on the ground on cold rainy nights? Would he have to worry about where he was going to find something to eat? I'm pretty sure your answer is that you would provide for all his needs. That doesn't mean treating him like a king, but all of his basic needs.

Jesus himself told us that if we seek first God's kingdom and his righteousness, his Father will meet all of our needs...

> *"Look at the birds of the air; they do not sow or reap or store away in barns, and yet your heavenly Father feeds them. Are you not much more valuable than they?" - Matthew 6:26 (NIV)*

> *"So do not worry, saying, 'What shall we eat?' or 'What shall we drink?' or 'What shall we wear?' For the pagans run after all these things, and your*

heavenly Father knows that you need them. But seek first his kingdom and his righteousness, and all these things will be given to you as well." - Matthew 6:31-33 (NIV)

Of course Jesus sought first God's kingdom and his righteousness, so he was speaking from experience.

I have heard, though I have not personally sought to verify it, that Jesus spoke more about finances than any other single topic. Among many other things, he said...

Give, and you will receive. Your gift will return to you in full - pressed down, shaken together to make room for more, running over, and poured into your lap. The amount you give will determine the amount you get back. - Luke 6:38 (NLT)

Does that sound like advice from a penniless, homeless man? Who would have listened to and followed his financial advice if he were homeless and poverty stricken? Would you? If a homeless man who sleeps under a bridge and wears shoddy clothes sought to offer you financial advice, I suspect you would quickly turn your back on him and walk away.

So, where do people get the idea that Jesus was homeless? Can you think of some place in the Bible that says he didn't have a home or a place to stay? Whenever I ask that question, someone is certain to volunteer a snippet from the gospel of Matthew where Jesus said...

The Angel of the Lord — Who Is He?

*"Foxes have dens to live in, and birds have nests, but
the Son of Man has no place even to lay his head." –
Matthew 8:20 (NLT)*

But that is only a small part of the story! The whole story is told in
Luke chapter 9, beginning at verse 51 (NLT)...

*As the time drew near for him to ascend to heaven,
Jesus resolutely set out for Jerusalem. He sent
messengers ahead to a Samaritan village to prepare
for his arrival. But the people of the village did not
welcome Jesus because he was on his way to
Jerusalem. When James and John saw this, they said
to Jesus, "Lord, should we call down fire from heaven
to burn them up?" But Jesus turned and rebuked
them. So they went on to another village. As they were
walking along, someone said to Jesus, "I will follow
you wherever you go." But Jesus replied, "Foxes
have dens to live in, and birds have nests, but the Son
of Man has no place even to lay his head." – Luke
9:51-58*

To put this singular incident into perspective it helps to know that
Jesus and his disciples were on their way to Jerusalem to
participate in the annual Jewish Passover celebration and that they
were traveling through Samaria. Jews, in general, hated Samaritans
and the feeling was mutual. So here was a Jewish Rabbi and his
disciples seeking to rent accommodations at the local guest house
in a small Samaritan village, and the proprietor would not rent to
them. Jesus and his disciples were probably tired and hungry; they
had walked a long way, and now the owner of the guest house

refused to let them stay there. So, they would need to walk on to another village and hope they would be welcome there. While they were walking to the next town, a seminary professor came up to Jesus and said: *"I will follow you wherever you go."* Jesus' reply was basically, "Really? I don't even have a place to sleep."

Now, knowing where people got the misconception that Jesus was poor and homeless, let's re-evaluate some things the Bible says about Jesus and his parents:

Born in a stable

Mary was pregnant with Jesus by the Holy Spirit. She was engaged to be married to Joseph. The Roman emperor Caesar Augustus ordered that a census be taken. Because of Joseph's family's lineage he was required to go to Bethlehem to be registered. When they arrived, Joseph sought accommodations at the local guest house, but **because of the census the guest house had no vacancy**. Mary went into labor, so they took refuge in a stable where she gave birth to baby Jesus.

> *And while they were there, the time came for her baby to be born. She gave birth to her first child, a son. She wrapped him snugly in strips of cloth and laid him in a manger, **because there was no lodging available for them**. - Luke 2:6-7(NLT)*

God provided for their escape to Egypt

Of course, God knew that King Herod was going to try to kill baby Jesus, and that Mary and Joseph would need to flee from Bethlehem. He knew they would need money for the trip and the means to support themselves, at least temporarily, when they got to where they were going.

So, God sent some wealthy men (the Wise Men) to give Mary and Joseph valuable gifts - gold, frankincense (an aromatic gum resin used in incense) and Myrrh (an essential oil used in perfume and to anoint dead bodies). Each of these was a commodity that could easily be converted to cash.

Tradition has the Wise Men (or Magi) worshipping Jesus in the stable, but that is not accurate because by the time they arrived the family was living in a house. It is reasonable to presume that they were either renting the house or a room in the house. Joseph was a professional craftsman, not a deadbeat. By the way, we don't know how many Wise Men there were. Three is only a guess that comes from the record of the three gifts that are mentioned in the Bible.

> *After this interview* (with King Herod) *the wise men went their way. And the star they had seen in the east guided them to Bethlehem. It went ahead of them and stopped over the place where the child was. When they saw the star, they were filled with joy!* **They entered the house** *and saw the child with his mother, Mary, and they bowed down and worshiped him. Then they opened their treasure chests and gave him gifts of gold, frankincense and myrrh. - Matthew 2:9-11 (NLT)*

Jesus - A master builder

The adult Jesus was a builder/craftsman like his father. We all know that an affable, honest, conscientious and skilled craftsman usually has all the work he can handle, and Jesus most certainly would have fit that description. I know I would want Jesus to build my house, wouldn't you? It is reasonable to assume that he made a good living and even had some money saved for the future.

Come and See

At the beginning of his approximately 3 years of ministry, Jesus was walking by the Jordan River where John the Baptist was preaching and baptizing people.

> *As Jesus walked by, John looked at him and declared, "Look! There is the Lamb of God." When John's two disciples heard this, they followed Jesus. Jesus looked around and saw them following. "What do you want?" he asked them. They replied, "Rabbi, where are you staying?" "Come and see," he said. It was about four o'clock in the afternoon when they went with him to the place where he was staying, and they remained with him the rest of the day. - John 1:36-39 (NLT)*

Note that Jesus didn't say he was homeless. He said, "Come and see." Most likely he was staying in someone's home or a guest house.

He had financial supporters

Naturally, when he began his three years of ministry leading up to his crucifixion, his income as a builder stopped. Some of his followers then provided support for him and his disciples.

> *Soon afterward Jesus began a tour of the nearby towns and villages, preaching and announcing the*

*Good News about the Kingdom of God. He took his
twelve disciples with him, along with some women
who had been cured of evil spirits and diseases.
Among them were Mary Magdalene, from whom he
had cast out seven demons; Joanna, the wife of
Chuza, Herod's business manager; Susanna;* **and
many others who were contributing from their own
resources to support Jesus and his disciples.** *Luke
8:1-3 (NLT)*

They even appointed a treasurer to handle finances (Judas). Who
knew? (Of course, Jesus did.)

*When Judas had eaten the bread, Satan entered into
him. Then Jesus told him, "Hurry and do what you're
going to do." None of the others at the table knew
what Jesus meant. Since Judas was their treasurer,
some thought Jesus was telling him to go and pay for
the food or to give some money to the poor. - John
13:27-29 (NLT)*

Jesus wore nice clothes
When Jesus went before Pilate and was sentenced to death,
he was not wearing raggedy old clothes. Among other things,
he was wearing an upscale, seamless robe, woven in one
piece.

*When the soldiers had crucified Jesus, they divided
his clothes among the four of them. They also took his
robe, but it was seamless, woven in one piece from
top to bottom. So they said, "Rather than tearing it*

*apart, let's throw dice for it." This fulfilled the
Scripture that says, "They divided my garments
among themselves and threw dice for my clothing." -
John 19:23-24 (NLT)*

The next time you hear someone says that Jesus was poor and
homeless, I hope you will disagree with them. God provided for all
of Jesus' needs, just as he will provide for all of your needs if you
follow his financial advice and trust in him to do so. How can
anyone expect you to believe that God wants to take good care of
you if he didn't take good care of his own son?

A history of God's generosity

The Bible tells us that if we trust in Jesus for our salvation, we
have the right to be called children of God. And God loves to bless
his children.

- Abraham was a very rich man with large herds of sheep, goats
  and cattle…because God blessed him.
- Abraham's son Isaac inherited his father's wealth.
- Isaacs son, Jacob, had to flee after he cheated his brother Esau
  out of his birthright, but God blessed him in the land he fled to,
  and he returned home years later a very rich man with a big
  family and large herds of sheep, goats and cattle.
- Jacob's son, Joseph, was appointed to rule over all of Egypt with
  only Pharaoh himself to report to. We can presume he was also
  wealthy.
- The Bible tells us that David was a man after God's own heart.
  God blessed David and made him king over Israel and Judah.
- David's son Solomon pleased God by asking for wisdom to
  rule wisely over God's people. As a result, God gave him
  outstanding wisdom and blessed him with unbelievable wealth.

- We are told that Job was blameless – a man of complete integrity. *He feared God and stayed away from evil. – Job 1:1* The Bible also tells us that he was the richest person in the entire area with 7,000 sheep, 3,000 camels, 500 teams of oxen, and 500 female donkeys!

Chapter 9

Just Like Us

True God and True Man

When I'm waiting in the doctor's office or while my car is being serviced, I frequently pick up one of the tabloid magazines. They have a lot of pictures, mostly of celebrities.

I always think it's funny when I see a section that says, "They're Just Like Us." Then they show a famous celebrity taking out the garbage, and another in a grocery store.

Well of course they take out the garbage and buy groceries just like we do. In fact, they have the same bathroom habits as we do, even occasional diarrhea (sorry). They are self-conscious when they have a big pimple on their nose. They get depressed and disappointed, and sometimes they cry.

But for some reason many people think that Jesus was not just like us. At times we've wondered about Jesus' childhood. Maybe you've pictured a beautiful baby who cooed, gurgled, and smiled all the time - or a toddler who was always content, only needing to be told "no" once, never spilling his milk or resisting potty training. If we think of Jesus that way, I think we miss the beautiful simplicity of God's plan.

Even though he was born without a sinful nature, he was still a human being and must have suffered all of the ailments, hurts, frustrations, anger, embarrassments and indignities that are common to human beings.

I think we can more fully appreciate what Jesus did for us when we understand that, while he walked the earth, he did so as a man. He did not have a little switch he could flip whenever he chose to use his God power.

While Samson's future mother described the angel of the Lord as looking "like an angel of God, very awesome," (Judges 13:6) the prophet Isaiah prophetically describes the coming Messiah, Jesus, this way...

> *He had no beauty or majesty to attract us to him,*
> *nothing in his appearance that we should desire him.*
> *- Isaiah 53:2*

I was told that the average Jewish man's height at Jesus' time was about 5'3". We know he had a beard because the Roman soldiers pulled out the hairs of his beard. We have another clue as to his appearance from an Old Testament prophecy about the coming Messiah...

> *His eyes will be darker than wine, his teeth whiter*
> *than milk. - Genesis 49:12*

So, if you've pictured a tall, handsome Jesus, you were probably wrong. Given Jesus' Bedouin ancestry he was probably an average looking, short Jewish man with brown to black hair and beard, with dark brown eyes and olive skin. God was definitely not looking to impress us with his Son's majesty. Quite the opposite.

The Angel of the Lord — Who Is He?

He was born in a stable not a palace, and road triumphantly into Jerusalem on a humble donkey, not a snorting, pawing white stallion.

While Jesus was most certainly true God and true man, the very success of his visitation to earth depended on his setting aside his deity until our salvation had been won. We're told that Jesus...

> *Who, being in very nature God, did not consider equality with God something to be used to his own advantage; rather, he made himself nothing by taking the very nature of a servant, being made in human likeness. And being found in appearance as a man, he humbled himself by becoming obedient to death - even death on a cross! – Philippians 2:6-7 (NIV)*

As with all things God sets out to do, he is successful. He decided to take on the very nature of a servant - to be made in human likeness. There is no hint in these words that his plan was to come in his power and glory *disguised* as a human. The Scripture says, "...but made himself *nothing...*" Nothing, just as we are nothing compared to God, *except for one important difference;* he would NOT take on our sinful nature. He made himself a sinless human being, the way he made Adam and Eve, with the same ability to choose between obeying God and giving in to the temptations of Satan.

I see a sense of divine fairness here, don't you? The Bible says...

> *"For just as through the disobedience of one man (Adam) the many were made sinners, so also through*

the obedience of one man (Jesus), *the many will be
made righteous."* - *Romans 5:19 (NIV)*

If God had come to earth without setting aside his deity, he would
have been immune to temptation, for we know that...

"God cannot be tempted by evil..." – James 1:13 (NIV)

Adam and Eve were condemned because they chose to disobey
God. I believe Jesus had to succeed where Adam and Eve failed,
having the same sinless nature, but the same susceptibility to
temptation. If the same nature was not enough for Jesus, God
might be accused of having expected too much from Adam and
Eve. The Bible tells us...

*" For we do not have a high priest who is unable to
sympathize with our weaknesses, but we have one
who has been tempted in every way, just as we are -
yet was without sin." Hebrews 4:15 (NIV)*

Of course baby Jesus was like every other baby and went through
the normal stages of child development! He messed his diapers
and didn't concern himself with what mommy wanted because, like
all babies, he thought he was the center of the universe (only in his
case he wasn't wrong like the rest of us). He may even have gone
through the "Terrible Twos." Are tantrums sinful? Or are they a
natural part of learning that we cannot always have things our own
way? I'll leave that conclusion to you.

The Angel of the Lord — Who Is He?

Is it hard to think of a young Jesus crying because some kids told him they didn't want him around? Is it hard to think of your Lord with embarrassing pimples?

When Jesus was twelve, he went with his parents and other relatives to Jerusalem to celebrate the feast of the Passover. They made this trip each year. A day into their return home, his parents realized that Jesus was not in their entourage of relatives and friends so they turned around and headed back to Jerusalem. Is it too difficult to read this story and realize that this was simply an adolescent behaving irresponsibly, just as every adolescent does now and then?

Humans learn responsibility. The 12-year-old Jesus probably gave no thought about how worried his parents would be. When he realized what he had put them through, I imagine he felt guilty. I'm confident he knew better the next time. An adolescent behaving irresponsibly is human nature, not sin.

In a prophecy about the Messiah the prophet Isaiah writes...

> *"...before the boy knows enough to reject the wrong*
> *and choose the right..." – Isaiah 7:16 (NIV)*

Luke writes that the 12-year-old Jesus amazed the teachers in the temple with his understanding and answers. There is no need to interpret Jesus' knowledge as a display of the omniscience of God. It is probable that Mary had told her son of the angel's visitation, of the circumstances surrounding his birth and the great promises concerning *him,* the promised Messiah. Jewish boys Jesus' age studied the Scriptures, and even memorized the Torah (the first five book of the Bible), but Jesus' knowledge of his divine heritage and his life's mission would logically have driven him to devour the Scriptures with an obsessiveness unmatched by other Jewish boys his age. He needed to know God's plan of salvation and *his* role as the promised Messiah. This alone would explain why the teachers in the temple were so impressed with his learning.

Isn't it good to know that our High Priest, Jesus, personally experienced our frustrations, embarrassments, nervousness, sadness, disappointments and every other feeling common to us humans? Aren't you glad that when you tell him you are sad, lonely or afraid, you're speaking to one who personally experienced those same feelings? In the book of Hebrews, chapter 2 we read...

> *"For this reason he had to be made like his brothers in every way, in order that he might become a merciful and faithful high priest in service to God, and that he might make atonement for the sins of the people. Because he himself suffered when he was tempted, he is able to help those who are being tempted." – Hebrews 2:17-18 (NIV)*

Chapter 10

Jesus' Miracles

But what about the miracles Jesus did? Don't they prove he had access to the power of God? Yes! Absolutely! Jesus did miracles by the power of the Holy Spirit. In the book of Acts we read...

> *Men of Israel, listen to this: Jesus of Nazareth was a man accredited by God to you by miracles, wonders and signs, which God did among you <u>through</u> him, as you yourselves know. – Acts 2:22 (NIV)*

Also, the Gospel of John says...

> *For the one whom God has sent speaks the words of God, to him God gives the Spirit without limit. – John 3:34 (NIV)*

But when, precisely, did this powerful anointing of the Holy Spirit come upon him. From all indications he did not have that special anointing when he was growing up.

Though the scriptures do not say anything about Jesus' earthly father, Joseph, after Jesus was 12 years old, most people presume that Joseph died sometime prior to the beginning of Jesus' ministry. Jesus was the son of God, yet apparently, he could not prevent his own father's death. No doubt he grieved for him. The Bible tells us that Jesus was, "a man of sorrows, acquainted with deepest grief." – Isaiah 53:3 (NLT)

The Angel of the Lord — Who Is He?

In the Gospel of John we read that...

> *"...even his* (Jesus') *own brothers did not believe in him." – John 7:5*

John isn't using "brothers" here as in the brotherhood of believers; he's referring to Mary's other sons who grew up with him. If Jesus had always had the power to perform miracles, certainly his own brothers would have acknowledged that he was not an ordinary man.

How is it that Jesus, who was God made flesh, didn't know the day or hour of his own return? His disciples asked him when he would return to earth to establish his kingdom, and Jesus responded...

> *"No one knows that day or hour, not even the angels in heaven, <u>nor the Son</u>, but only the Father." – Matthew 24:36*

Have you wondered why the Gospel writer Mark records that when Jesus was in his hometown of Galilee,

> *"He could not do any miracles there except to lay his hands on a few sick people and heal them. And he was amazed at their lack of faith"? – Mark 6:5-6*

A well-meaning writer of Bible footnotes commented that Jesus *could* have done miracles there, but he chose not to because of their little faith. I think, in this instance, it's better to let the Scriptures say what they say, and that is, "He <u>could not</u> do any miracles there.

In Luke chapter 3 we read...

> *"When all the people were being baptized, Jesus was baptized, too. And as he was praying, heaven was opened and **the Holy Spirit descended on him in bodily form like a dove**. And a voice came from heaven, 'You are my Son, whom I love; with you I am well pleased.'" – Luke 3:21-22 NIV*

In chapter 1 of the Gospel of John we get more details about this event...

> *"Then John* (the Baptist) *gave this testimony: 'I saw the Spirit come down from heaven as a dove **and remain on him**.'" – John 1:32 (NIV)*

In the next verse he goes on to say...

> *"I would not have known him except that the one who sent me to baptize with water* (God) *told me, 'The man on whom you see the Spirit come down **and remain** is he who will baptize with the Holy Spirit.'" – John 1:33 (NIV)*

THIS WAS THE PRECISE MOMENT when a powerful anointing of the Holy Spirit came upon Jesus in the Jordan River!

In Luke, chapter 4, Luke tells us that immediately after Jesus' baptism…

> *"Jesus, **full of the Holy Spirit**, returned from the Jordan and was led by the Spirit in the desert, where for forty days he was tempted by the devil." – Luke 4:1-2 (NIV)*

Let's not deceive ourselves into thinking that Satan's temptations were wasted on Jesus because he was the Son of God. The person being tempted was Jesus *the man!* - who had chosen to humble himself in this way. We can be sure that he was intensely tempted by the master of temptations! Let's also remember we should never feel guilty when we are bombarded with temptations. Being tempted is not sin. Sin is *giving in* to temptation. Had Jesus yielded to even one of the devil's temptations, he would not have been the unblemished sacrifice that was needed to take away our sin. Satan would have won a mighty victory, just as he did in the Garden of Eden.

Jesus' temptations were not limited to those forty days in the desert; they were a part of his life just as they are a part of ours. In verse 13 we read...

> *"When the devil had finished all this tempting, he left him until an opportune time." - Luke 4:13 (NIV)*

In the very next verse we read...

> *"Jesus returned to Galilee **in the power of the Spirit**" – Luke 4:14 (NIV)*

The Angel of the Lord — Who Is He?

Shortly after the Holy Spirit came upon him in the Jordan River, we read in John chapter 2 about Jesus attending a wedding in Cana where he miraculously turned water into wine. We are told...

> *"This, **the first of his miraculous signs** (changing water into wine), Jesus performed in Cana in Galilee" – John 2:11 (NIV)*

In Luke 4 we read about Jesus in the synagogue in Nazareth. The scroll of the prophet Isaiah was handed to him. Jesus unrolled it and read the Scripture prescribed for the day...

> *"**The Spirit of the Lord is on me**, because he has anointed me to preach good news to the poor. He has sent me to proclaim freedom for the prisoners and recovery of sight for the blind, to release the oppressed, to proclaim the year of the Lord's favor."* – Luke 4:18-19 (NIV)

Then he rolled up the scroll and said...

> *"Today this scripture is fulfilled in your hearing."* – Luke 4:21 (NIV)

A brief chronological recap
1. Jesus' own brothers don't believe in him
2. Jesus is baptized by John the Baptist in the Jordan River; the Holy Spirit descends on him, and remains
3. Immediately, Jesus, full of the Holy Spirit, is led by the Spirit into the wilderness to be tempted by Satan
4. Jesus returns to Galilee in the power of the Spirit

5 Jesus turns water into wine, at the wedding in Cana; his first miracle
6 Jesus reads from the scroll of Isaiah in the temple... *"The Spirit of the Lord is upon me, because he has anointed me to preach good news to the poor."*

The following brief encounter convinced disciple-to-be Nathaniel that Jesus had abilities beyond those of an average human. It is significant to note that this encounter occurred when Jesus was beginning to choose some men to be his disciples, and that this was *after* his baptism by John in the Jordan River when the Holy Spirit descended upon Jesus and remained on him...

Philip found Nathanael and told him, "We have found the one Moses wrote about in the Law, and about whom the prophets also wrote—Jesus of Nazareth, the son of Joseph." "Nazareth! Can anything good come from there?" Nathanael asked. "Come and see," said Philip. When Jesus saw Nathanael approaching, he said of him, "Here truly is an Israelite in whom there is no deceit." "How do you know me?" Nathanael asked. Jesus answered, "I saw you while you were still under the fig tree before Philip called you." Then Nathanael declared, "Rabbi, you are the Son of God; you are the king of Israel." Jesus said, "You believe because I told you I saw you under the fig tree. You will see greater things than that." He then added, "Very truly I tell you, you will see 'heaven open, and the angels of God ascending and descending on the Son of Man." - John 1:45-51 (NIV)

Jesus acknowledged the source of his power. He said...

> *"The Son can do nothing by himself; he can only do what he sees his Father doing." – John 5:19 NIV*

> *"By myself I can do nothing; I judge only as I hear, and my judgment is just, for I seek not to please myself but him who sent me." – John 5:30 NIV*

And finally, we read...

> *"For the one whom God has sent speaks the words of God; to him God gives the Spirit without limit." – John 3:34 NIV*

The Spirit of God is the source of power! – both for Jesus and for us. The Spirit will empower us too if we would learn to yield to him completely as Jesus did. Jesus said so...

> *"I tell you the truth, anyone who has faith in me will do what I have been doing. He will do even greater things than these, because I am going to the Father." – John 14:12 NIV*

Jesus' prayer life is a shining example for us. He spent many hours and sometimes all night in prayer to our Father in heaven. We can't even imagine the blessings and power that God would entrust to us if we committed our lives to his will and cultivated our personal relationship with him as Jesus did.

Chapter 11

*"My God, my God,
Why Have You Forsaken Me?"*

Have you wondered why Jesus cried out on the cross,

> *My God, my God, why have you forsaken me? –
> Matthew 27:46 (NIV)*

The common explanation is that Jesus was quoting verse 1 of
Psalm 22. I don't know about you, but that doesn't ring true in my
spirit. Here is a man in excruciating pain; he has been beaten
mercilessly and is now hanging on a cross from heavy spikes
driven through his wrists and feet - quoting Scriptures. Consider
this: Jesus was not quoting Psalm 22, rather Psalm 22 is quoting
Jesus! The Psalmist, David, inspired by the Holy Spirit,
prophetically recorded words and thoughts of Jesus as he hung on
the cross many centuries later.

See if you don't agree that the following descriptions in Psalm 22
are of Jesus on the cross...

> *I am poured out like water, and all my bones are out
> of joint. My heart has turned to wax; it has melted
> within me. My mouth is dried up like a potsherd, and
> my tongue sticks to the roof of my mouth; you lay me
> in the dust of death. Dogs surround me, a pack of
> villains encircles me; they pierce my hands and my*

feet. All my bones are on display; people stare and gloat over me. They divide my clothes among them and cast lots for my garment. But you, LORD, do not be far from me. You are my strength; come quickly to help me. - Psalm 22:14-19 (NIV)

Surely you recognize this description of Jesus' crucifixion from the New Testament accounts, right down to the Roman soldiers throwing dice to determine who would get his seamless robe. Dogs would typically be at the foot of a cross licking up the blood dripping from the one impaled on it.

When he cried out...

"My God, my God, why have you forsaken me?"

...it was the voice of a man racked with unimaginable pain, desperate for it to end!

Jesus knew well every prophecy about how he would be abused, humiliated, and crucified. He recently had said...

"Now my heart is troubled, and what shall I say? 'Father, save me from this hour?' No, it was for this very reason I came to this hour. Father, glorify your name." – John 12:27-28 - (NIV)

However, a short while later, in the Garden of Gethsemane, we see Jesus' full humanity on display when he pleads with God the Father three times for permission to not go through with what was about to happen. Overwhelmed by fear and anxiety over what he knew was imminent, he pleaded with God for a last-minute reprieve...

> *"Going a little farther he fell to the ground and prayed that, if possible, the hour might pass from him. 'Abba, Father,' he said, 'everything is possible for you. Take this cup from me. Yet not what I will, but what you will.'" – Mark 14:35-36 (NIV)*

Oh, how the heart of God must have been pierced by the pleas of his beloved Son. Even in despair, Jesus was ready to obey his Father's will though it meant horrible pain and suffering.

> *Once more he went away and prayed the same thing." – Mark 14:39 (NIV)*

> *So he left them and went away to pray the third time, saying the same thing. – Matthew 26:44*

In anguish, he implored God to provide another way. Although he knew what his Father desired him to do, he also knew the choice was his. His Father had told him so.

> *The reason my Father loves me is that I lay down my life – only to take it up again. No one takes it from me, but I lay it down of my own accord. I have authority to lay it down and authority to take it up again. This command I received from my Father. – John 10:17-18 (NIV)*

How Satan pressed him to side-step the ultimate mission for which he came to earth. The choice was his, but he needed the Father to say it was okay not to go through with it. His Father would not. He could not, there was too much at stake.

Then they came for him. Even as he was being arrested, he reminded everyone that his Father would honor whatever choice he made...

> *"Do you think I cannot call on my Father, and he will at once put at my disposal more than twelve legions of angels?" – Matthew 26:53 (NIV)*

If only Adam and Eve's desire to do God's will in the Garden of Eden had been as strong, all this would have been unnecessary.

The hours that followed saw Jesus insulted vilely and ridiculed. The Bible tells us that he was blindfolded, mocked and beaten. Guards slapped him, spit in his face, pulled out the hairs of his beard, pummeled him with their fists, and repeatedly struck him on the head with a staff. A crown of thorns was pressed onto his head. The creator of the universe endured it all for our sakes!

Pontius Pilate orders the dreaded Roman flogging

In John Pollock's book, The Master – A Life of Jesus, he writes: "He (Peter) watched the soldiers strip Jesus naked and bend him over the pillar, tying him so that back, buttocks, and legs were equally exposed. Two burly slaves stood ready, also naked. Each picked up a whip of three leather thongs on which had been strung lumps of bone, and standing on either side of him, they brought down the whips in turn with all their might, to cut through skin, nerves, and muscle. They lashed the shoulders and spinal cord, his buttocks and his thighs. Thongs curled round and cut his chest and ribs. A flogging with the flagellum could kill in itself if prolonged, or cripple for life; but a man to be crucified must be left the strength to carry the crossbeam to the site of execution. The pain was atrocious... When the flogging stopped and they unbound him and he stood in his blood, shivering from shock, cut and bruised from shoulders to calves, they mocked him."

Then Jesus was led away to be crucified – a slow and excruciatingly painful death. Since shame and affront to human dignity were part of the punishment, he was no doubt stripped naked before the throng of onlookers. Heavy iron spikes were driven through his hands and feet, or more likely his wrists and feet. We can't even imagine the agony – his open wounds from the brutal flogging pressed against the rough wood of the cross, muscle cramps, the spikes, flies, thirst, difficulty in breathing, the jeers and mockery.

Jesus hung there for hours in unbearable pain. The choice was still his. Legions of angels stood ready to rescue him, but the request was not made. When would the Father rescue him with the sweet death he longed for? Wasn't it enough yet? He pleaded...

> *"Oh my Strength, come quickly to help me"* – *Psalm 22:19 (NIV)*

In utter torment and despair he cried out,

> *"My God, my God, why have you forsaken me?"* – *Matthew 15:34 (NIV)*

74

His loving Father had turned away from his precious Son; his heart must have been tortured with his own pain. What father or mother could stand by and watch their innocent child obediently accept such atrocities? Finally, the dreadful price had been fully paid for all humanity. It was enough! His distraught Father granted the death his dear Son longed for.

> *Then Jesus shouted, Father, I entrust my spirit into your hands!" And with those words he breathed his last. - Luke 23:46 (NLT)*

It is written...

> *"And being found in appearance as a man, he humbled himself and became obedient to death – even death on a cross! Therefore, God exalted him to the highest place and gave him the name that is above every name, that at the name of Jesus, every knee should bow, in heaven and on earth, and every tongue confess that Jesus Christ is Lord, to the glory of God the Father." – Philippians 2:8-11 (NIV)*

After his resurrection, Jesus' disciples asked him again when he would set up his kingdom. This time his answer was different.

> *"It is not for <u>you</u> to know the times or dates the Father has set by his own authority." – Acts 1:7*

He was no longer a mortal man. He again knew all things and shared the glory he had with the Father before the creation of the world.

What a glorious day it will be when Jesus returns for those whom he purchased with his blood - when we look upon his face.

> *"They will see the Son of Man coming on the clouds of the sky, with power and great glory. And he will send his angels with a loud trumpet call, and they will gather his elect from the four winds, from one end of the heavens to the other."* – Matthew 24:30-31(NIV)

Thank you, dear Father, for loving us so much that you sent your one and only Son to redeem us. Thank you, dear Jesus, for your obedience to our Father's will, though it meant unspeakable suffering in my place. And thank you, Holy Spirit, for bringing me to the knowledge of my salvation and for keeping me firm in my faith that Jesus paid the full price for my sins.

Chapter 12

Why Did Jesus Have to Die?

We Are All Sinners

Besides for Adam and Eve before the fall, the only ones mentioned in the Bible who are sinless, is God the Father and God the Son, Jesus Christ.

Abraham, Isaac and Jacob of the Old Testament, along with Mary, Saint Peter and Saint Paul in the New Testament, were all sinners like you and me.

Saint Paul, who is credited with writing more than half of the books in the New Testament by the inspiration of the Holy Spirit, had this to say about himself:

> *"And I know that nothing good lives in me, that is, in my sinful nature. I want to do what is right, but I can't. I want to do what is good, but I don't. I don't want to do what is wrong, but I do it anyway. But if I do what I don't want to do, I am not really the one doing wrong; it is sin living in me that does it. I have discovered this principle of life – that when I want to do what is right, I inevitably do what is wrong. I love God's law with all my heart. But there is another power within me that is at war with my mind. This power makes me a slave to the sin that is still within me. Oh, what a miserable person I am! Who will free*

me from this life that is dominated by sin and death?"
– Romans 7:18-24 (NLT))

Then he answers his own question.

"Thank God! The answer is in Jesus Christ our
Lord." – Romans 7:25 (NLT)

We might call Paul a "holy" man of God from the perspective that he was chosen by God and set apart to preach and teach the Word of God. But we cannot call him sinless. By his own admission he was not.

We are all born with a nature that will lead us to sin. We are called to be holy, that is, we are challenged to live blameless lives with the help of the Holy Spirit who lives within us; however, God does not expect us to live without sin. He knows we cannot. That's why he sent his blameless Son to pay the full price for our sins. Because of Jesus' sacrifice, God sees those who have chosen to make Jesus the Lord of their lives as righteous in his sight! His Word tells us that he has removed our sins from us as far as the east is from the west. He sees us as sinless!

We cannot do anything to earn God's love and forgiveness. It is a free gift from a loving and merciful God.

God saved you by his grace when you believed. And
you can't take credit for this; it is a gift from God.
Salvation is not a reward for the good things we have
done, so none of us can boast about it. – Ephesians
2:8-9 (NLT)

78

In other words, God didn't say, "Clean up your act and then come see me." He paid for our sins himself and then invites us to receive his free gift of eternal life by trusting in his Son's sacrifice as full payment for our sins.

What the Bible does and does not say

Even though the Bible is clear that we are saved by faith, so many people seem unable to grasp this.

When asked if they are going to heaven when they die, a huge percentage of the population will either say they don't know, or respond in terms of how good or kind or generous they have been. They miss the whole point of God's message.

So here are some Bible verses along with some non-Bible verses that might be helpful in driving home the reality of God's grace (undeserved love).

The Bible says: *For God loved the world so much that he gave his one and only Son, so that everyone who believes in him will not perish but have eternal life. – John 3:16 (NLT)*

It does *not* say: For God loved the world so much that he gave his one and only Son to teach us how we must live so we will not perish but have eternal life.

The Bible says: *God saved you by his grace when you believed. And you can't take credit for this; it is a gift from God. Salvation is not a reward for the good things we have done, so none of us can boast about it. – Ephesians 2:8-9 (NLT)*

It does *not* say: You are saved when you keep God's laws and commandments and do what is right. Salvation is a reward for the good things you have done.

The Bible says: *The wages of sin is death, but the free gift of God is eternal life through Christ Jesus our Lord. – Romans 6:23 (NLT)*

It does *not* say: The wages of sin is death, but those who live a Godly life will be rewarded with eternal life.

The Bible says: (Jesus speaking) *"Now go and learn the meaning of this Scripture; 'I want you to show mercy, not offer sacrifices.' For I have not come to call those who think they are righteous, but those who know they are sinners." – Matthew 9:13 (NLT)*

It does *not* say: "Now go and learn the meaning of this Scripture; 'I want you to offer sacrifices and do what is right.' For I have not come to call those who are sinners, but those who are righteous."

The Bible says: (Jesus speaking) *"O Jerusalem, Jerusalem, the city that kills the prophets and stones God's messengers! How often I have wanted to gather your children together as a hen protects her chicks beneath her wings, but you wouldn't let me." – Matthew 23:37 (NLT)*

It does *not* say: "O Jerusalem, Jerusalem, the city that kills the prophets and stones God's messengers! How often I have wanted to destroy you because of your hard hearts, but I spared you.

The Bible says: *Don't you see how wonderfully kind, tolerant, and patient God is with you? Does this mean nothing to you? Can't you see that his kindness is intended to turn you from your sin? – Romans 2:4 (NLT)*

It does *not* say: Don't you know that God is a righteous, just and demanding God? Does this mean nothing to you? Can't you see that his discipline and punishments are intended to turn you from your sin?

The Bible says: *The LORD says, "I will rescue those who love me. I will protect those who trust in my name. When they call on me, I will answer; I will be with them in trouble. I will rescue and honor them. I will reward them with a long life and give them my salvation." – Psalm 91:14-16 (NLT)*

It does *not* say: The LORD says, "I will rescue those who please me by living honorably. When they call on me, I will answer; I will be with them in trouble. I will rescue and honor them. I will reward them with a long life and give them my salvation."

The Bible says: *O Lord, you are so good, so ready to forgive, so full of unfailing love for all who ask for your help. Listen closely to my prayer, O LORD; hear my urgent cry. I will call to you whenever I'm in trouble, and you will answer me. - Psalm 86:5-7 (NLT)*

It does *not* say: I, the Lord your God, am a Holy God who does not tolerate the sinful acts of men. They will not go unpunished.

Chapter 13

Can We Ever Be Sure of Our Salvation?

So many people are uncertain about their salvation. Jesus paid the full penalty for our sins, and there is nothing more we can do to make ourselves right with God.

But then we read in the Bible,

> *Don't you realize that those who do wrong will not inherit the Kingdom of God? Don't fool yourselves. Those who indulge in sexual sin, or who worship idols, or commit adultery, or are male prostitutes, or practice homosexuality, or are thieves or greedy people, or drunkards, or are abusive, or cheat people – none of these will inherit the Kingdom of God. – 1 Corinthians 6:9-10 (NLT)*

…and we again begin to question our salvation. Are we good enough? But that is not the right question.

St. Paul continues…

> *Some of you were once like that. But you were cleansed; you were made holy; you were made right with God by calling on the name of the Lord Jesus Christ and by the Spirit of God. – 1 Corinthians 6:11 (NLT)*

So, our sins are forgiven no matter how bad they were, but what about the sins we continue to commit? Certainly we cannot *willfully* continue to sin and expect God to continue to forgive us, can we? No, we cannot. We will all continue to sin as long as we live in these sinful, earthly bodies, but when we do so *willfully*, we need to sincerely repent and confess that sin. Confession is nothing more than acknowledging to God that we did something wrong and asking for forgiveness. If our confession and repentance are sincere, God will never fail to forgive us and restore the relationship we violated by our willfulness. On the other hand...

> *Dear friends, if we deliberately continue sinning after we have received knowledge of the truth, there is no longer any sacrifice that will cover these sins. There is only the terrible expectation of God's judgment and the raging fire that will consume his enemies. -* Hebrews 10:26-27 (NLT)

The Bible tells us that believing in Jesus Christ gives us the right to be called God's children and the right to go to his throne and talk to him in prayer the way a son or daughter talks to a father whom they know loves them. That new relationship is intended to last forever. Jesus said he will never allow Satan to snatch us out of his hands.

A Relationship Much Like God's Institution of Marriage

In a way it is like the institution of marriage. When we leave the altar, we are married. It's official! The new relationship is intended to be permanent. The marital relationship will inevitably experience its ups and downs. There are times we will offend our spouse. Perhaps we will forget our partner's birthday or become so engrossed in other things that we cease to spend personal time with him or her. We may make our partner jealous or angry by something we do. We may even be unfaithful to our partner and cause great offense. BUT, through it all we continue to be married; we continue to be in that special relationship. If we are sorry for our shortcomings, and if our partner has a forgiving nature like God does, he or she will forgive us for all the things we do wrong, and will continue to love us. The relationship remains unbroken.

At the moment we cross "the faith threshold" and believe that Jesus died for our sins and confess him as Lord, the Holy Spirit takes up residence inside of us. At that instant we have entered into a saving relationship with God that is very much like the marital relationship. God knows there will be ups and downs. We will offend him. We may make him jealous by the way we use our time and the things we make our priorities. We may fall into sins of the flesh. We may even be completely unfaithful to him for a time, but the relationship continues. We have not lost our salvation! God will patiently work to draw us to repentance because he wants the relationship to remain intact. The only way God will give up on the relationship is if we no longer value it. If we insist on going our own way and refuse to work at the relationship there will come a time that his patience will run out...and his Holy Spirit will leave us. We will have broken the relationship by showing our contempt for it.

I like to say that we need to make Jesus "the Lord of our life." What that means to me is that not only do we trust in his death on the cross as full payment for our sins, but we also seek to please him in our daily lives because we are no longer our own, he bought us with the price of his precious blood. We owe him everything.

So, the answer to the question, "Can We Ever Be Sure of Our Salvation?" is a resounding, "Yes! Absolutely!" If we make Jesus the Lord of our life, we will spend eternity with him. Our continuing failures to live without sin will not be held against us because Jesus paid the whole penalty for those sins. God sees us as blameless, washed by the blood of his Son.

> *Now all glory to God, who is able to keep you from falling away and will bring you with great joy into his glorious presence without a single fault. – Jude vs. 24 (NLT)*

Chapter 14

Justification

When a person is justified with God, it means that he or she has been forgiven and made right with him. We are justified with God by our faith that his Son's sacrifice was full payment for our sins, and recognizing that we cannot contribute to that justification in any way.

> *God saved you by his grace when you believed. And you can't take credit for this; it is a gift from God. Salvation is not a reward for the good things we have done, so none of us can boast about it. - Ephesians 2:8-9 (NLT)*

Nearly everyone, including me, has a hard time internalizing the enormity of God's grace, mercy, love and compassion. Except for Christianity, every other religion in the world requires a person to do good works to appease a judgmental God and turn away his wrath. But the one true God found in the Bible is not at all like that. The following Bible Scriptures affirm this truth repeatedly...

> *Then the LORD came down in a cloud and stood there with him (Moses); and he called out his own name, Yahweh. The LORD passed in front of Moses, calling out, "Yahweh! The LORD! The God of compassion and mercy! I am slow to anger and filled with unfailing love and faithfulness. I lavish unfailing love*

to a thousand generations. I forgive iniquity, rebellion, and sin. - Exodus 34:5-7 (NLT)

I will thank you, Lord, among all the people. I will sing your praises among the nations. For your unfailing love is as high as the heavens. Your faithfulness reaches to the clouds. - Psalm 57:9-10 (NLT)

For God loved the world so much that he gave his one and only Son, so that everyone who believes in him will not perish but have eternal life. God sent his Son into the world not to judge the world, but to save the world through him. There is no judgment against anyone who believes in him. But anyone who does not believe in him has already been judged for not believing in God's one and only Son. - John 3:16-18 (NLT)

We are made right with God by placing our faith in Jesus Christ. And this is true for everyone who believes, no matter who we are. - Romans 3:22 (NLT)

Can we boast, then, that we have done anything to be accepted by God? No, because our acquittal is not based on obeying the law. It is based on faith. So we are made right with God through faith and not by obeying the law. - Romans 3:27-28 (NLT)

For the Scriptures tell us, "Abraham believed God, and God counted him as righteous because of his faith." When people work, their wages are not a gift, but something they have earned. But people are counted as righteous, not because of their work, but because of their faith in God who forgives sinners. - Romans 4:3-5 (NLT)

Therefore, since we have been made right in God's sight by faith, we have peace with God because of what Jesus Christ our Lord has done for us. Because of our faith, Christ has brought us into this place of undeserved privilege where we now stand, and we confidently and joyfully look forward to sharing God's glory. - Romans 5:1-2 (NLT)

And since we have been made right in God's sight by the blood of Christ, he will certainly save us from God's condemnation. - Romans 5:9 (NLT)

For the wages of sin is death, but the free gift of God is eternal life through Christ Jesus our Lord. - Romans 6:23 (NLT)

If you confess with your mouth that Jesus is Lord and believe in your heart that God raised him from the dead, you will be saved. For it is by believing in your heart that you are made right with God, and it is by confessing with your mouth that you are saved. - Romans 10:9-10 (NLT)

For God made Christ, who never sinned, to be the offering for our sin, so that we could be made right with God through Christ. - 2 Corinthians 5:21 (NLT)

I do not treat the grace of God as meaningless. For if keeping the law could make us right with God, then there was no need for Christ to die. - Galatians 2:21 (NLT)

But - "When God our Savior revealed his kindness and love, he saved us, not because of the righteous things we had done, but because of his mercy. He washed away our sins, giving us a new birth and new life through the Holy Spirit. He generously poured out the Spirit upon us through Jesus Christ our Savior. Because of his grace he declared us righteous and gave us confidence that we will inherit eternal life." - Titus 3:4-7 (NLT)

Chapter 15

After We Are Justified God Begins to Sanctify Us

In the previous chapter we were assured that anyone who has made Jesus the Lord of their life has eternal life. Does that mean it is okay for Christians to engage in all of the same sinful behaviors as those who do not know God? No, it isn't, but as the previous chapter makes clear, we do not clean up our act, so to speak, and then come to God, rather we come to God and he then helps us clean up our act.

God's Holy Spirit draws true Christians away from willfully engaging in those behaviors that his Word tells us displease him. Does that mean that over time we will become perfect human beings? Of course not, we will always fall short as long as we live in these sinful bodies, but as we grow in our knowledge of God <u>from reading and/or hearing his Word</u>, our behaviors will begin to conform more and more to what we know pleases him. This process is known as ***Sanctification***.

The fruits of our sinful nature are:

- Sexual immorality (sexual sin) including adultery and practicing homosexuality, pedophilia, etc. (Leviticus 18)
- Idolatry, sorcery, voodoo
- Hostility, outbursts of anger, quarreling, abusiveness

- Greed, cheating, stealing
- Jealousy, envy, selfish ambition
- Lying
- Drunkenness and lack of self-control

The fruits of the Spirit are:

- Love
- Joy
- Peace
- Patience
- Kindness
- Goodness
- Faithfulness
- Gentleness
- Self-control

Don't copy the behavior and customs of this world, but let God transform you into a new person by changing the way you think. Then you will learn to know God's will for you, which is good and pleasing and perfect. - Romans 12:2 (NLT)

So I say, let the Holy Spirit guide your lives. Then you won't be doing what your sinful nature craves. The sinful nature wants to do evil, which is just the opposite of what the Spirit wants. And the Spirit gives us desires that are the opposite of what the sinful nature desires. These two forces are constantly fighting each other, so you are not free to carry out your good intentions. But when you are directed by the Spirit, you are not under obligation to the law of Moses. - Galatians 5:16-18 (NLT)

And I will give you a new heart, and I will put a new spirit in you. I will take out your stony, stubborn heart and give you a tender, responsive heart. And I will put my Spirit in you so that you will follow my decrees and be careful to obey my regulations. - Ezekiel 36:26-27 (NLT)

Those who are dominated by the sinful nature think about sinful things, but those who are controlled by the Holy Spirit think about things that please the Spirit. So letting your sinful nature control your mind leads to death. But letting the Spirit control your mind leads to life and peace. For the sinful nature is always hostile to God. It never did obey God's laws, and it never will. That's why those who are still under the control of their sinful nature can never please God. But you are not controlled by your sinful nature. You are controlled by the Spirit if you have the Spirit of God living in you. (And remember that those who do not have the Spirit of Christ living in them do not belong to him at all.) - Romans 8:5-9 (NLT)

Therefore, dear brothers and sisters, you have no obligation to do what your sinful nature urges you to do. For if you live by its dictates, you will die. But if through the power of the Spirit you put to death the deeds of your sinful nature, you will live. - Romans 8:12-13 (NLT)

For once you were full of darkness, but now you have light from the Lord. So live as people of light! For this light within you produces only what is good and right and true. Carefully determine what pleases the Lord. Take no part in the worthless deeds of evil and darkness; instead, expose them. - Ephesians 5:8-11 (NLT)

So you must live as God's obedient children. Don't slip back into your old ways of living to satisfy your own desires. You didn't know any better then. But now you must be holy in everything you do, just as God who chose you is holy. For the Scriptures say, "You must be holy because I am holy." - 1 Peter 1:14-16 (NLT)

Sanctification is a process initiated by the Holy Spirit. Our goal should be to be holy because our God is holy; however, the reality is that our actions will never be completely holy as long as we are living in a sinful body. Thank God that he sees us as blameless because of our faith in Jesus' sacrificial death. The Bible tells us that our sins have been removed from us a far as the east is from the west. We can't get any holier than that.

Chapter 16

The Glory That Awaits Us

We have all seen a depiction of a boy or girl with wings and a halo, supposedly in heaven; typically, he or she is sitting on a cloud and playing a harp. Yawn. Boring.

In this chapter we will look at passages that suggest a life after death that is anything but boring.

I believe that John chapter 17 (which we previously addressed), sometimes known as Jesus' High Priestly Prayer, gives us a clue as to what lies ahead for the believer. To refresh your memory, Jesus knows he is soon to be arrested and crucified. He prays…

> *"I have brought you glory on earth by finishing the work you gave me to do. And now, Father, glorify me in your presence with the glory I had with you before the world began." John 17:4-5 - (NIV)*

> *"Father, I want those you have given me to be with me where I am, and to see my glory, the glory you have given me because you loved me before the creation of the world. – John 17:24*

My personal belief is that, in a way similar to the way God the Father shared his glory with the angel of the Lord (Jesus), God intends to share his glory with those of us who have made Jesus the Lord of our lives. To what degree that might be, is a complete unknown. We are told...

> *I consider that our present sufferings are not worthy comparing with **the glory that will be revealed in us**. – Romans 8:18 NIV*

> *Dear friends, now we are children of God, and what we will be has not yet been made known. But we know that when he appears, **we shall be like him**, for we shall see him as he is. - 1 John 3:2 NIV*

> *Do you not know that **the saints will judge the world**? And if you are to judge the world, are you not competent to judge trivial cases? Do you not know that **we will judge angels?** – 1 Corinthians 6:2-3 NIV*

Degrees of rewards in heaven

The Bible tells us that there will be degrees of rewards in heaven. In the Old Testament book of Daniel, the mighty angel that appeared to Daniel prophesied to him about end times, that is, about when the Messiah (Jesus) returns on judgement day...

> *"At that time Michael, the great prince who protects your people, will arise. There will be a time of distress such as has not happened from the beginning of nations until then. But at that time your people—everyone whose name is found written in the book—will be delivered. Multitudes who sleep in the dust of the earth will awake: some to everlasting life, others to shame and everlasting contempt. **Those who are wise will shine like the brightness of the***

*heavens, and **those who lead many to righteousness, like the stars for ever and ever.***" *- Daniel 12:1-3 (NIV)*

Everyone who honors Jesus as Lord, and trusts in his suffering and death as full payment for their sins, will be saved; however, some will receive great rewards for eternity, and apparently some will get into heaven by the skin of their teeth. Or as St. Paul says...

...he himself will be saved, but only as one escaping through the flames. - 1 Corinthians 3:15 (NIV)

Here are more references to rewards in heaven...

"Blessed are you when people insult you, persecute you and falsely say all kinds of evil against you because of me. Rejoice and be glad, because great is your reward in heaven." - Matthew 5:11–12 (NIV)

"But store up for yourselves treasures in heaven, where moth and rust do not destroy, and where thieves do not break in and steal. For where your treasure is, there your heart will be also." - Matthew 6:20 (NIV)

"For we must all appear before the judgment seat of Christ, that each one may receive what is due him for the things done while in the body, whether good or bad." - 2 Corinthians 5:10 (NIV)

"Be careful not to practice your righteousness in front of others to be seen by them. If you do, you will

*have no reward from your Father in heaven. So when
you give to the needy, do not announce it with
trumpets, as the hypocrites do in the synagogues and
on the streets, to be honored by others. Truly I tell
you, they have received their reward in full. But when
you give to the needy, do not let your left hand know
what your right hand is doing, so that your giving
may be in secret. Then your Father, who sees what is
done in secret, will reward you. And when you pray,
do not be like the hypocrites, for they love to pray
standing in the synagogues and on the street corners
to be seen by others. Truly I tell you, they have
received their reward in full. But when you pray, go
into your room, close the door and pray to your
Father, who is unseen. Then your Father, who sees
what is done in secret, will reward you." - Matthew
6:1-6 (NIV)*

While we are saved by God's grace through faith in Jesus
Christ, what we do now on this earth counts for all eternity!
Rather than be focused on earthly things, such as the
accumulation of wealth or the approval of others, we ought to
be focused on God's approval.

In the parable of the talents, Jesus tells the story of a man who
entrusts his property to his servants before going on a long journey.
To one he gave five talents, to another two talents, and to a third he
gave one talent. I've read somewhere that a talent, in Jesus' time,
may have been worth about $400,000 U.S. dollars. Regardless of
the value, the servant who received five talents doubled the money
entrusted to him, as did the servant who had received two. The

third servant, however, did nothing to further his master's interests; he buried his master's money in the ground. When the master returned, he rewarded each of the two faithful servants with the words...

> *"Well done, good and faithful servant! You have been faithful with a few things; I will put you in charge of many things. Come and share your master's happiness!" - Matthew 25:23 (NIV)*

The lazy servant who did nothing with the talent given to him was thrown out unceremoniously. May none who read these words end up as that man.

What will we do in heaven?

We may not always think so, but work is a blessing from God. Working at something we enjoy, and are good at, is fulfilling. When God created Adam, he gave him responsibilities, among which were tending the Garden of Eden and naming all of the animals. So, it's safe to say we will all be given responsibilities. Just above we read the words of the master to his faithful servants...

> *"Well done, good and faithful servant! You have been faithful with a few things; **I will put you in charge of many things.** Come and share your master's happiness!" – Matthew 5:23 (NIV)*

Whatever God has in store for you, you can be sure it won't be boring. He knows what you enjoy doing, and what you will find fulfilling. You won't need to learn to play the harp, unless you want to.

You have probably heard it said that planet earth, compared to all of the planets and stars in the universe, is the equivalent of one grain of sand on all the beaches of the world. I suppose for this reason many suspect that there must be life on other planets. It does seem somewhat egotistical to assume we are the only life forms in the universe. If there is life on other planets, our God created them, as he did us, so not to worry. The possibilities of what God has planned for us are unlimited. Perhaps you will be like God to a life form that inhabits a planet in a galaxy far, far away. Or not.

> *No eye has seen, no ear has heard, no mind has*
> *conceived what God has prepared for those who love*
> *him... - 1 Corinthians 2:9 (NIV)*

Kenneth March is an ordained Christian minister, an evangelist and missionary. He has been a missionary to the Philippines and Africa.

He was the founder and CEO of a 501(c)(3) non-profit, Haiti mission society for 25 years, personally in Haiti more than 40 times, including conducting week-long seminary classes for pastoral students.

Ken is currently the President of a non-profit international mission society.

Kenneth's email address is: *KennethMarch@rocketmail.com*

You may also be interested in Kenneth March's book: *MISLED - Is God Calling His People to Leave the Roman Catholic Church?*, available in English, Italian, Spanish, Portuguese and French.

Made in the USA
Las Vegas, NV
24 December 2023

83160559R00056